SPOT-THE-DIFFERENCE ARCHITECTURE | 40 BRAIN-BENDING PHOTOGRAPHIC PUZZLES

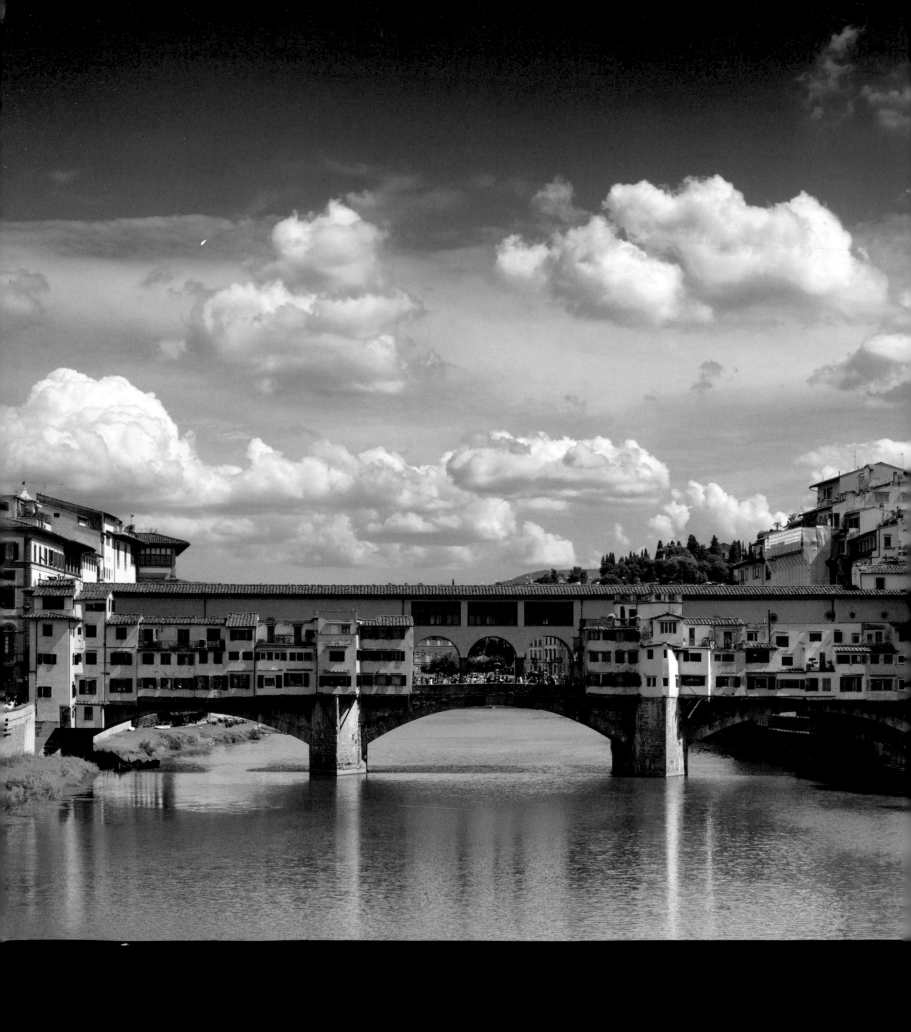

An amazing
passport-free
world trip
for challenge
seekers

SPOT-THE-DIFFERENCE ARCHITECTURE | 40 BRAIN-BENDING PHOTOGRAPHIC PUZZLES

PUZZLE
WRIGHT
PRESS
New York

PUZZLE WRIGHT PRESS

New York

An Imprint of Sterling Publishing Co., Inc.
1166 Avenue of the Americas
New York, NY 10036

© 2018 Octopus Publishing Group
This Puzzlewright edition published in 2018.

ISBN 978-1-4549-3186-7

Distributed in Canada by Sterling Publishing Co., Inc.
c/o Canadian Manda Group, 664 Annette Street
Toronto, Ontario, Canada M6S 2C8

For information about custom editions, special sales,
and premium and corporate purchases, please contact
Sterling Special Sales at 800-805-5489 or
specialsales@sterlingpublishing.com.

Manufactured in China

www.sterlingpublishing.com
www.puzzlewright.com

Image credits: **Alamy Stock Photo** Eric Lafforgue 66;
Eye Ubiquitous 40; Sean Pavone 46. **Dreamstime.com**
Irina Burakova 54; Alxcrs 52; Claudiodivizia 62; Diego
Grandi 10; Eugenesergeev 86; Frederic Prochasson 50;
Lerka555 56; Luis Sandoval Mandujano 48; Meunierd 82;
minnystock 30; Nicola Messana 38; Pixattitude
12; Sarah Dusautoir 20; Stuart Monk 22; Yulan 44. **Getty
Images** Arthit Somsakul 28; Benjawan Sittidech 26.
iStockphoto.com 06photo 16; 3D_generator 34; Badahos
78; bjdlzx 70; efired 42; Jorisvo 68; klug-photo 64;
littleny 36; mazzzur 76; Nikada 58; OscarCatt 60; phant
18; Rafal Cichawa 24; RuslanKaln 14; rusm 80; sfe-co2 8;
somchaisom 32 & front cover; TerryJ 84; tverkhovinets
74; Will Selarep 72.

Concept and images from The Art Archive Ltd.

CONTENTS

INTRODUCTION 6

ROKUON-JI Kyoto, Japan 8

PAINTED LADIES San Francisco, USA 10

CHURCH OF SAINT FRANCIS OF ASSISI Ouro Preto, Brazil 12

TOPKAPI PALACE Istanbul, Turkey 14

FORBIDDEN CITY Beijing, China 16

SAINT PETER'S BASILICA Vatican City 18

PALACE OF VERSAILLES Versailles, France 20

CHRYSLER BUILDING New York City, USA 22

LAS LAJAS SANCTUARY Ipiales, Colombia 24

FLINDERS STREET STATION Melbourne, Australia 26

SAINT BASIL'S CATHEDRAL
(CATHEDRAL OF VASILY THE BLESSED) Moscow, Russia 28

NEUSCHWANSTEIN CASTLE Bavaria, Germany 30

TAJ MAHAL Agra, India 32

ELIZABETH TOWER, PALACE OF WESTMINSTER
London, UK 34

PARIS LAS VEGAS Las Vegas, USA 36

SHAH-I-ZINDA MAUSOLEUM Samarkand, Uzbekistan 38

INNTEL HOTEL ZAANDAM Zaandam, The Netherlands 40

PONTE VECCHIO Florence, Italy 42

CASTELLO DI SAMMEZZANO Reggello, Italy 44

WAT BENCHAMABOPHIT (THE MARBLE TEMPLE)
Bangkok, Thailand 46

CENTRAL LIBRARY, NATIONAL AUTONOMOUS
UNIVERSITY OF MEXICO Mexico City, Mexico 48

PENA PALACE Sintra, Portugal 50

CHÂTEAU DE CHAMBORD Chambord, France 52

WINTER PALACE Saint Petersburg, Russia 54

CHURCH OF THE SAVIOR ON SPILLED BLOOD
Saint Petersburg, Russia 56

CASA BATLLÓ Barcelona, Spain 58

FLORENCE DUOMO (CATHEDRAL OF SAINT MARY
OF THE FLOWER) Florence, Italy 60

BARBICAN CENTRE London, UK 62

HAGIA SOPHIA Istanbul, Turkey 64

BUQSHAN HOTEL Khaila, Yemen 66

MYSORE PALACE Mysore, India 68

JINGMING TOWER, SUMMER PALACE Beijing, China 70

ALHAMBRA Granada, Spain 72

SAINT MICHAEL'S GOLDEN-DOMED MONASTERY Kiev, Ukraine 74

DANCING HOUSE Prague, Czech Republic 76

SHEIKH ZAYED GRAND MOSQUE Abu Dhabi, UAE 78

SAINT MARK'S BASILICA Venice, Italy 80

HABITAT 67 Montreal, Canada 82

DOME OF THE ROCK Old City, Jerusalem 84

NOTRE-DAME Paris, France 86

ANSWERS 88

INTRODUCTION

We often miss things when rushing from point A to point B, but the 40 architectural feats showcased in this book will stop you in your tracks and demand a closer look. Study your favorite iconic buildings and challenge yourself with 40 visual puzzles.

Each puzzle contains a total of 20 differences to spot—and the devil is in the detail. As you search for incongruities, the cunning design, materials, and creative decisions that contributed to each stunning result will be revealed. Taking a closer look will reward you with a deeper understanding of what makes these structures so masterful.

The answers are included at the back, and captions provide insight into each landmark, be it on the engineering, function, or philosophy behind the construction.

Take a trip around the globe, from Venice to Beijing, from London to New York. Marvel at the magnitude of the Taj Mahal, delight in the spectacular detail of Gaudí's façades, and be wowed by many more architectural treasures in this phenomenal photographic collection.

Each fun and fascinating title from this series of grown-up activity books combines the pleasure of puzzle-solving with the contemplative study of art and our environment.

ELIZABETH TOWER, PALACE OF WESTMINSTER
London, UK
1843–1859

This symbol of the United Kingdom was named after Queen Elizabeth II in 2012 in celebration of her Diamond Jubilee. Famously known as Big Ben, this is actually the name of the 13.5-ton bell contained within the clock itself. As the ground has shifted since its construction, partly as the result of the extension of a subway line underneath it, the tower leans by roughly 9 inches (23cm), which is just barely perceptible to someone at street level.

Answers to the puzzles
are in the back of the book:
follow the grid references
to discover the changes.

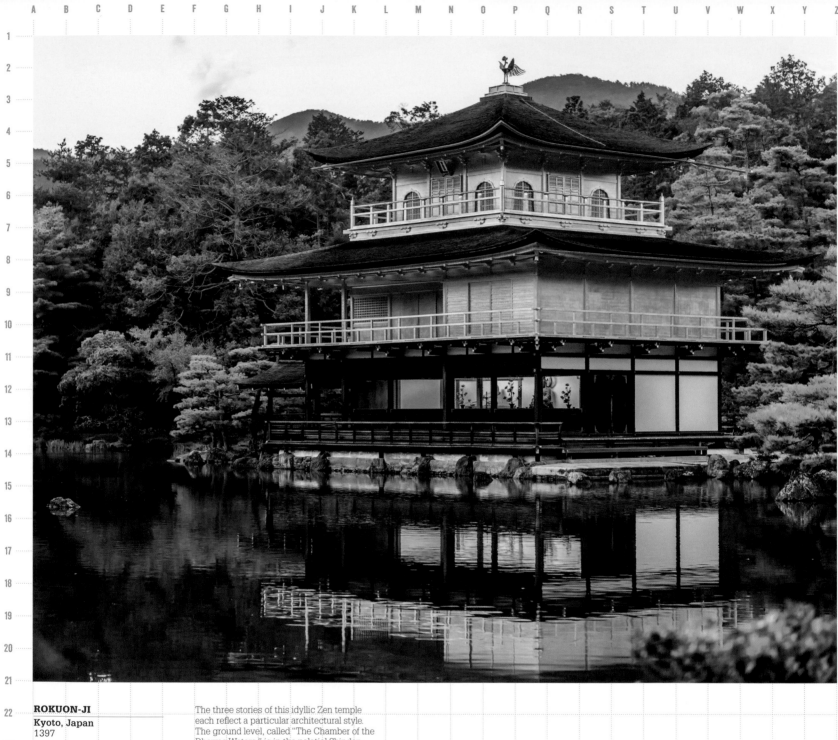

ROKUON-JI

Kyoto, Japan
1397

The three stories of this idyllic Zen temple each reflect a particular architectural style. The ground level, called "The Chamber of the Dharma Waters," is in the palatial Shinden-zukuri style, and is an open plan reflecting the surrounding gardens. The upper two stories, both covered in pure gold leaf, are called "The Tower of Sound Waves" and "The Cupola of the Ultimate." The former is in the samurai Buke-zukuri style, and contains a Buddha hall, and the small top story is in the traditional Zen style.

PAINTED LADIES

San Francisco, USA
1892–1896

These Victorian houses were always meant to attract attention, being in the flashy American Queen Anne style, complete with a dizzying combination of architectural features. But their iconic colors came about only in the 1960s, when artists in the colorist movement painted the façades in vivid hues, which were quickly adopted by neighboring hippies.

CHURCH OF SAINT FRANCIS OF ASSISI

Ouro Preto, Brazil
1766

The façade of this stunning example of Brazilian Baroque was designed by innovative architect, Aleijadinho. Its novel features include the circular bell towers, and the oculus at the top center, which encloses a stone relief depicting Saint Francis receiving his stigmata.

TOPKAPI PALACE
Istanbul, Turkey
1460–1478

This room sits beneath the Ottoman palace's largest dome. Surrounded by blue-and-white Delft tiles and Murano glass, and amid opulent gifts from European royalty, the Ottomon sultans would recline on this throne and enjoy the entertainment provided to them and their harem.

FORBIDDEN CITY

Beijing, China
1406–1420

So named because no one could enter or leave it without the Emperor's permission, this entire palace complex stretches out symmetrically along a central north-south axis, as an expression of the Confucian ideal of unifying humanity and nature. Hence the presence of the Hall of Supreme Harmony, the Hall of Central Harmony, and the Hall of Preserving Harmony, all along a single axis.

SAINT PETER'S BASILICA

Vatican City
1506–1626

The largest church in the world, Saint Peter's went through over a half-dozen architects before Michelangelo took on the job. He harmonized the disparate approaches of his predecessors, and is responsible for the construction of the impressive dome. Half a century later, however, Carlo Maderno added the current façade that, while in proportion when viewed from a distance (as shown above), obscures the bottom half of the dome when standing in the piazza directly in front of the church.

PALACE OF VERSAILLES
Versailles, France
1661–1715

Beginning its life as a simple hunting lodge, this extravagant royal palace was expanded by Louis XIV to be the architectural embodiment of French royalty, in both opulent and pragmatic ways. Amid the 700 lavishly decorated rooms and 3.1 square miles (8km^2) of gardens, the king could keep his nobles entertained and in check, all the while asserting his status as the center of their lives—quite literally, as the entire palace centers on the king's apartment.

CHRYSLER BUILDING

New York City, USA
1928–1930

An icon of Art Deco architecture as well as of Manhattan itself, this skyscraper was the tallest in the world for 11 months before it was eclipsed by the Empire State Building, with which it was in direct competition throughout its construction. In fact, its crowned spire was secretly assembled inside the frame of the tower, to be hoisted up through the top and completed in the span of just 90 minutes.

LAS LAJAS SANCTUARY
Ipiales, Colombia
1916–1949

This unusual location for a church, spanning a canyon in a remote site in the mountains, was not chosen for practical reasons. Legend has it that, in 1754, the Virgin Mary appeared on a vertical cliff high above the river to a mother and her daughter while they were taking shelter from a storm amid the *lajas* (the stones at the bottom of the valley).

FLINDERS STREET STATION

Melbourne, Australia
1905–1910

Australia's oldest train station is built in the French Renaissance style, with a magnificent dome as its centerpiece. It's such a common meeting point for Melburnians that "meet me under the clocks" is shorthand for rendezvousing at the front of the station, where distinctive clocks display the departure times.

SAINT BASIL'S CATHEDRAL (CATHEDRAL OF VASILY THE BLESSED)

Moscow, Russia
1555–1561

The unprecedented style of Saint Basil's has given rise to much historical speculation as to what influenced its design and how its construction was achieved. The colorful exterior, however, was only added a century after being built, and is derived from an evocative description of heaven found in the Book of Revelation.

NEUSCHWANSTEIN CASTLE

Bavaria, Germany
1869–1886

By the time Neuschwanstein was built, castles had long ceased serving as defensive fortifications. Rather, this castle-palace was meant as a fantastical escape for a king who's political power was steadily declining. King Ludwig II would go on to be nicknamed the "Fairy Tale King" (*der Märchenkönig*), which makes it all the more fitting that his castle inspired the Sleeping Beauty Castle in Disneyland, not to mention the Walt Disney Pictures logo.

TAJ MAHAL
Agra, India
1632–1653

Persian, Islamic, Turkic, and Indian styles blend together in this monumental mausoleum for an emperor's lost love. The marble is said to reflect the different moods of Shah Jahan's deceased wife—bright and sparkling white on a sunny day, warm and golden at dusk and dawn, or celestial and blue when reflecting the moonlight.

ELIZABETH TOWER, PALACE OF WESTMINSTER

London, UK
1843–1859

This symbol of the United Kingdom was named after Queen Elizabeth II in 2012 in celebration of her Diamond Jubilee. Famously known as Big Ben, this is actually the name of the 13.5-ton bell contained within the clock itself. As the ground has shifted since its construction, partly as the result of the extension of a subway line underneath it, the tower leans by roughly 9 inches (23cm), which is just barely perceptible to someone at street level.

PARIS LAS VEGAS
Las Vegas, USA
1997

Squeezing as much of the City of Lights as it can into a 24-acre plot of land, this landmark hotel and casino includes a two-thirds size Arc de Triomphe, two hotels in the style of the Paris Opera House and the Louvre, and a 1:2-scale replica of the Eiffel Tower itself.

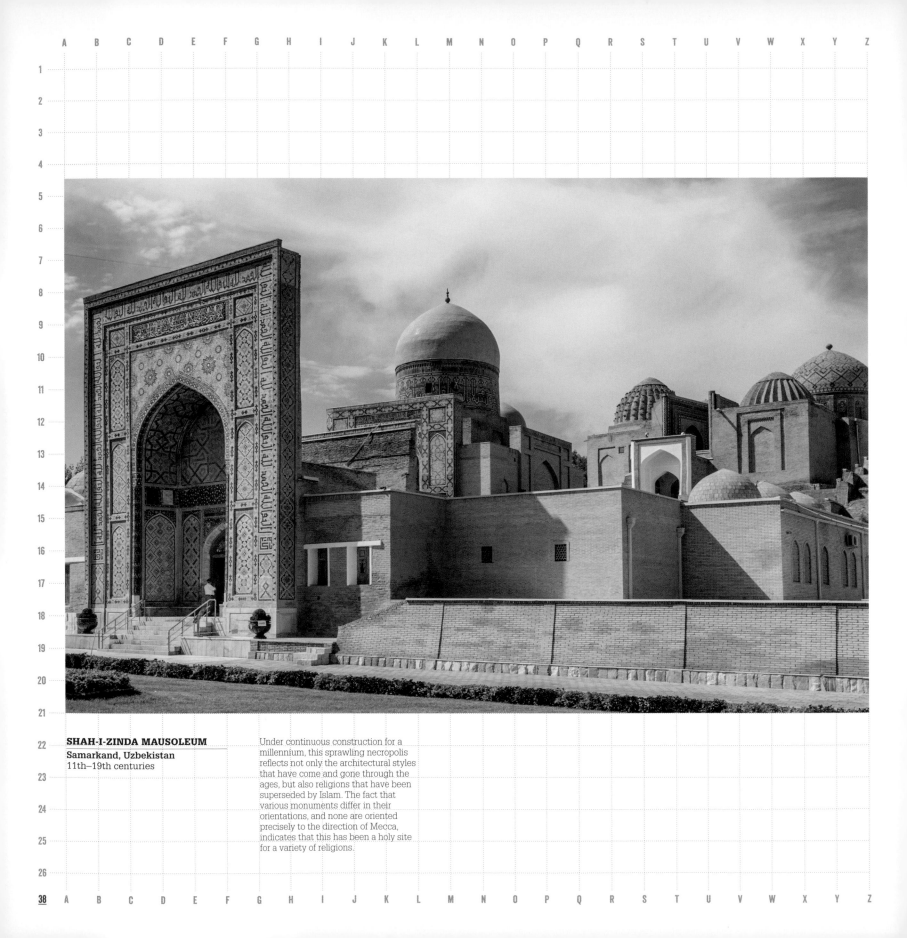

SHAH-I-ZINDA MAUSOLEUM

Samarkand, Uzbekistan
11th–19th centuries

Under continuous construction for a millennium, this sprawling necropolis reflects not only the architectural styles that have come and gone through the ages, but also religions that have been superseded by Islam. The fact that various monuments differ in their orientations, and none are oriented precisely to the direction of Mecca, indicates that this has been a holy site for a variety of religions.

INNTEL HOTEL ZAANDAM
Zaandam, The Netherlands
2010

This 11-story hotel combines the traditional architecture of Zaandam in an eccentric and attention-grabbing modern style. Almost 70 individual houses are stacked together to form the greater structure, all painted the traditional green of the Zaan region—with the exception of the blue house in the upper-left corner, which is a reference to *The Blue House at Zaandam*, painted by Claude Monet in 1871.

PONTE VECCHIO
Florence, Italy
1345

Two centuries after this bridge was first built, Duke Cosimo de' Medici wanted to move freely across the river between his residence at the Palazzo Pitti and the seat of government in the Uffizi. To avoid having to mix with the public, he had Giorgio Vasari build the Vasari Corridor—the long private passage stretching across the tops of all the stores along the span of the bridge.

CASTELLO DI SAMMEZZANO

Reggello, Italy
1605–1889

Following the 18th-century trend of Orientalism, Ferdinando Panciatichi Ximenes d'Aragona remodeled this lavish castle into a vivid example of the Moorish Revival style. The Latin words above the doors on either side (literally, "nothing more beyond") were originally meant as a warning to sailors that they were approaching the end of the world, but here they are an invitation for visitors to explore a colorful new world.

**WAT BENCHAMABOPHIT
(THE MARBLE TEMPLE)**

**Bangkok, Thailand
1899–1911**

Built to serve the Thai royal household,
this modern Buddhist temple is constructed
out of Italian Carrara marble, and houses
no fewer than 52 bronze statues of Buddha.
The Buddha collection is a mix of original
works and copies from a range of artistic
periods through Southeast-Asian Buddhist
art, including the famous Phra Phuttha
Chinnarat from Wat Yai in Northern Thailand.

**CENTRAL LIBRARY,
NATIONAL AUTONOMOUS
UNIVERSITY OF MEXICO**

Mexico City, Mexico
1956

The exterior of this repository of over 120,000 volumes is one of the largest murals in the world, and uses natural colored stone, rather than paint, to depict its subjects. Each wall tells a story of the history of Mexico through three eras—the ancient pre-Hispanic, the colonial Spanish, and the Modern.

PENA PALACE

Sintra, Portugal
1842–1854

Fully embracing the Romanticism of its era, this palace combines Renaissance, Moorish, Gothic, Manueline, and Baroque styles in a reflection of King Ferdinand II's personal tastes. The eclectic colors continue this amalgamation of disparate architectural features—with European medieval towers sitting alongside Islamic minarets. In viewing it, you may well be reminded of Neuschwanstein Castle, for which it served as an inspiration.

51

CHÂTEAU DE CHAMBORD

Chambord, France
1519–1547

When King Francis I wanted a fresh design for his château that would reflect the blossoming French Renaissance, he turned to none other than Leonardo da Vinci, who brought his experience and eccentricity to the drawing board (though the degree of his involvement is subject to scholarly debate). The roof is probably the most distinctive feature—it certainly was to Henry James, who wrote in his *A Little Tour in France*, that "the towers, cupolas, the gables, the lanterns, the chimneys, look more like the spires of a city than the salient points of a single building."

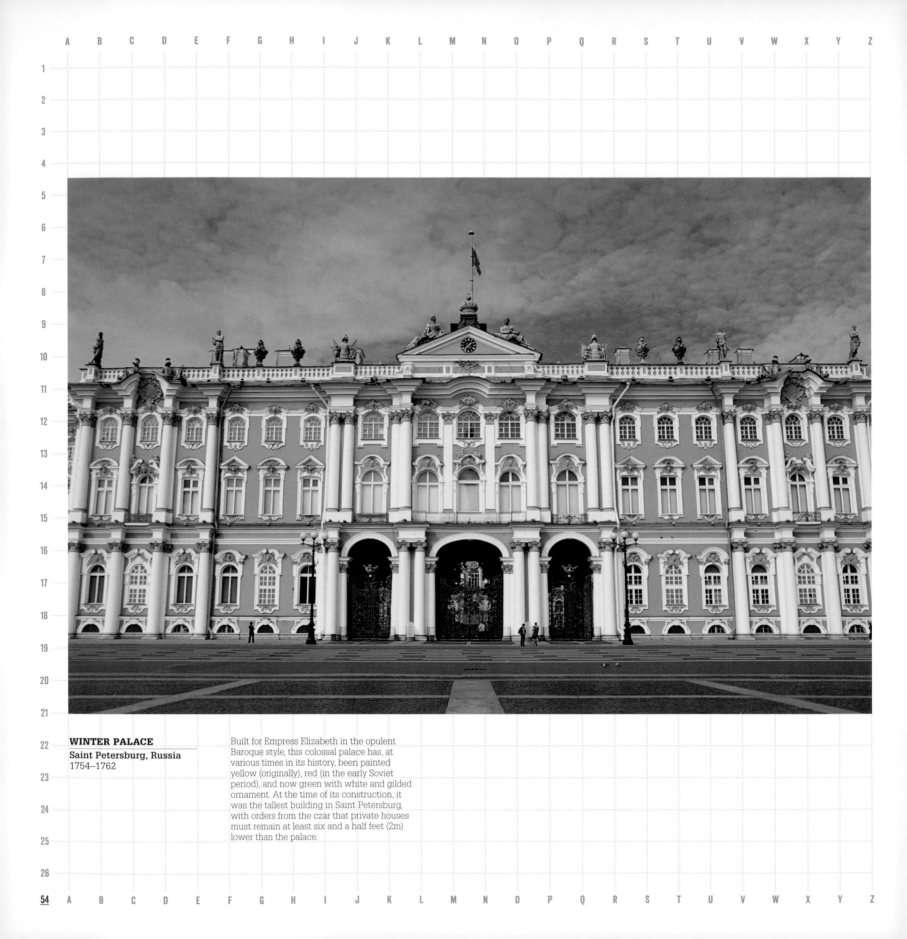

WINTER PALACE
Saint Petersburg, Russia
1754–1762

Built for Empress Elizabeth in the opulent Baroque style, this colossal palace has, at various times in its history, been painted yellow (originally), red (in the early Soviet period), and now green with white and gilded ornament. At the time of its construction, it was the tallest building in Saint Petersburg, with orders from the czar that private houses must remain at least six and a half feet (2m) lower than the palace.

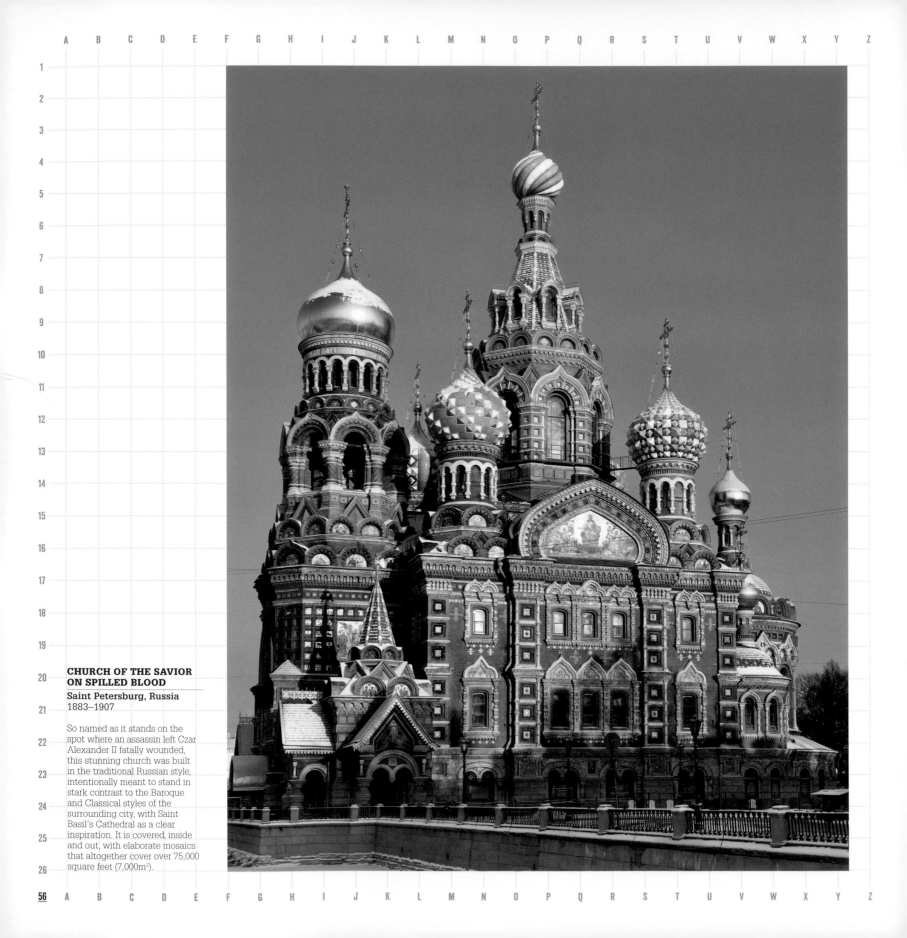

CHURCH OF THE SAVIOR ON SPILLED BLOOD

Saint Petersburg, Russia
1883–1907

So named as it stands on the spot where an assassin left Czar Alexander II fatally wounded, this stunning church was built in the traditional Russian style, intentionally meant to stand in stark contrast to the Baroque and Classical styles of the surrounding city, with Saint Basil's Cathedral as a clear inspiration. It is covered, inside and out, with elaborate mosaics that altogether cover over 75,000 square feet (7,000m²).

CASA BATLLÓ

Barcelona, Spain
1877–1906

Colloquially known as the House of Bones due to its skeletal features, this is one of Antoni Gaudí's best-known masterpieces. The building connects with the patron saint of its Catalan home via its architectural embellishments: the tiles of the organically curved roof represent the scales of a dragon, which has been subdued by the turret at the top left, itself representing Saint George's lance.

FLORENCE DUOMO (CATHEDRAL OF SAINT MARY OF THE FLOWER)

Florence, Italy
1296–1436

This was the largest dome in the world when it was built; no one had even come close since Rome built the Pantheon some 1,400 years earlier. And it had to be built, as the ambitious Florentines had already constructed the rest of the church, and the plans dictated the massive octagonal center could be covered by nothing else. After an intense competition, Filippo Brunelleschi won the commission and rose to the challenge, using construction techniques that have been lost to history and that puzzle architects to this very day.

BARBICAN CENTRE
London, UK
1971–1982

Brutalism rose to fashion after World War II as a modern ideal of urban design, and the Barbican stands as one of its foremost examples. Using raw concrete as its defining material, the center itself is a performing-arts venue, and, together with the surrounding estate, strives to weave together high-density housing with commercial and cultural areas to form a cohesive vision for how people should live in a growing metropolis.

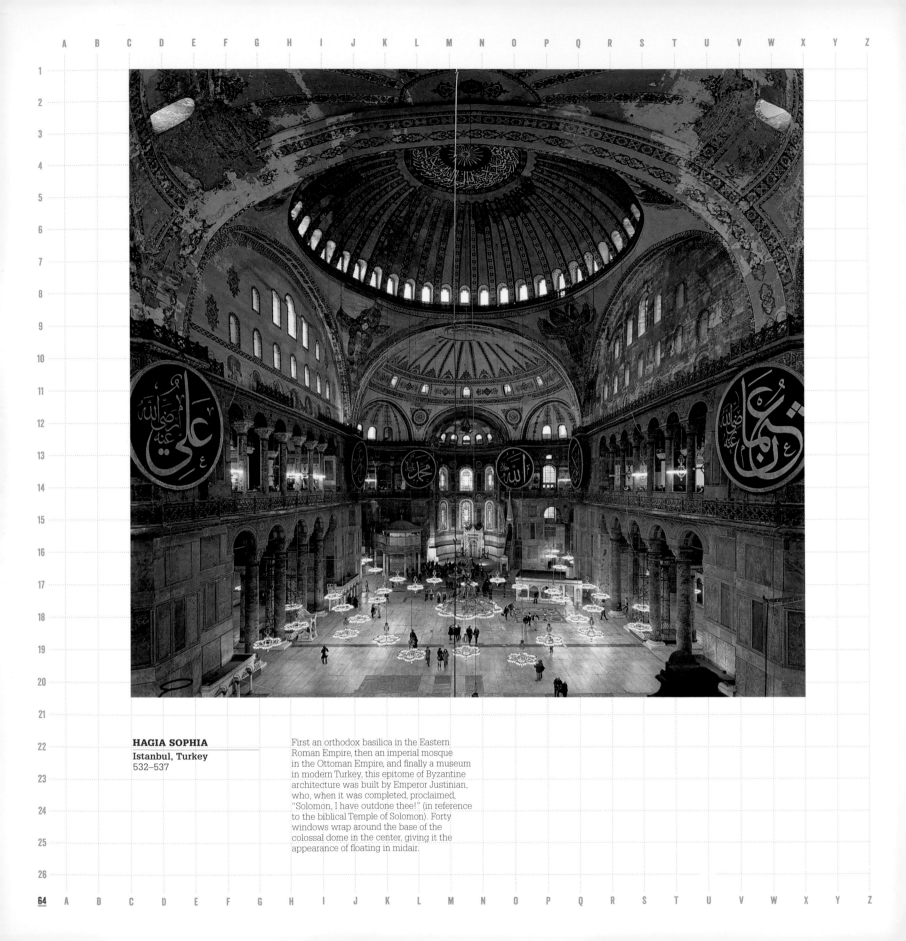

А B C D E F G H I J K L M N O P Q R S T U V W X Y Z

HAGIA SOPHIA
Istanbul, Turkey
532–537

First an orthodox basilica in the Eastern Roman Empire, then an imperial mosque in the Ottoman Empire, and finally a museum in modern Turkey, this epitome of Byzantine architecture was built by Emperor Justinian, who, when it was completed, proclaimed, "Solomon, I have outdone thee!" (in reference to the biblical Temple of Solomon). Forty windows wrap around the base of the colossal dome in the center, giving it the appearance of floating in midair.

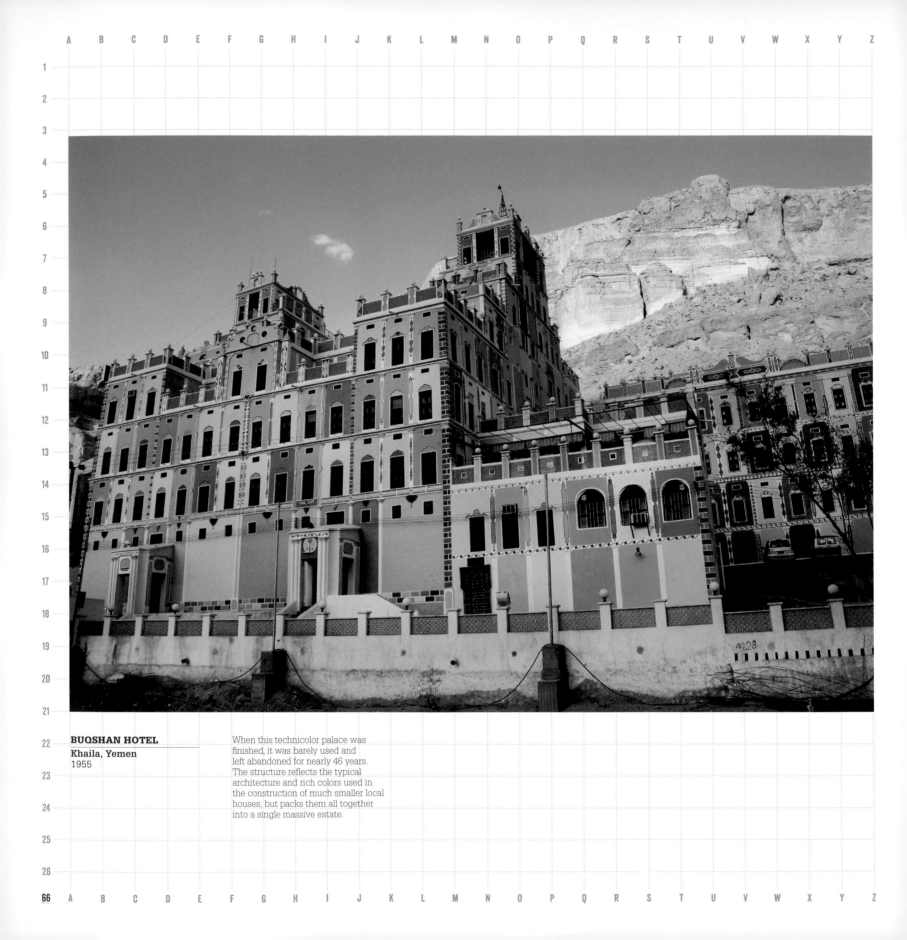

BUQSHAN HOTEL

Khaila, Yemen
1955

When this technicolor palace was finished, it was barely used and left abandoned for nearly 46 years. The structure reflects the typical architecture and rich colors used in the construction of much smaller local houses, but packs them all together into a single massive estate.

MYSORE PALACE

Mysore, India
1897–1912

This Indo-Saracenic palace complex blends Gothic, Rajput, Hindu, and Muslim architectural styles, including the 144-foot (44m) tower shown here. There are no fewer than 12 Hindu temples contained in the complex, each covered in intricately carved details, with the oldest dating to the 14th century.

JINGMING TOWER, SUMMER PALACE

Beijing, China
Jing Dynasty (1115–1234)

Built by the Qianlong Emperor to celebrate the birthday of his mother, the Summer Palace is a massive array of palaces arranged amid a series of lakes and gardens spanning 1.1 square miles (2.9km²). Using over 100,000 laborers, the emperor expanded and organized the natural lakes in the region into a cohesive vision, inspired by the Chinese version of the Fountain of Youth myth.

ALHAMBRA
Granada, Spain
1238

A mile (1.6km) of walls and 30 towers form the boundary of this fortified city-within-a-city, which functioned as a royal residence for the Nasrid dynasty of Muslim rulers in Spain, a barracks for their army, and a royal court. It evolved gradually over the centuries, incorporating native Andalusian features and embellished with ornate decorations like arabesques and exquisite tilework.

SAINT MICHAEL'S GOLDEN-DOMED MONASTERY

Kiev, Ukraine
1108–1999

This is the latest iteration of a monastery complex that has existed on this site since the early 12th century, most recently demolished by the Soviet Union but promptly rebuilt as a symbol of Ukrainian resilience. It retains its original fusion of Byzantine planning and Ukrainian Baroque flourishes, such as the vivid blue paint that contrasts brilliantly with the golden domes.

DANCING HOUSE

Prague, Czech Republic
1992–1996

Affectionately nicknamed "Fred and Ginger," this landmark of Deconstructivist architecture represents the famous actor and actress Fred Astaire and Ginger Rogers dancing together. The twisting shape is achieved with 99 separate concrete panels, each custom built to a precise shape that interlocks with all the rest.

SHEIKH ZAYED GRAND MOSQUE

Abu Dhabi, UAE
1996–2007

Built to be the main place of worship in the UAE, this expansive mosque can accommodate up to 41,000 people. Its design was meant to unite a vast array of different influences and styles, reflecting the diversity within the Islamic world. It contains the world's largest carpet, made in Iran, seven chandeliers with millions of Swarovski crystals, made in Germany, and a lighting system designed by British architects to reflect the surrounding pools onto the building itself.

SAINT MARK'S BASILICA

Venice, Italy
978–1092

This magnificent cathedral reflects not only Venice's wealth, with its gold-ground mosaics and intricate details, but also its global influence, with its fusion of Byzantine and Italian architectural styles. The four bronze horses seen here above the main entrance date back to Roman antiquity, and were part of the Hippodrome of Constantinople until Doge Enrico Dandolo took them back to Venice after the Fourth Crusade.

HABITAT 67
Montreal, Canada
1967

Constructed for the 1967 World's Fair (Expo 67), this sprawling residential complex is composed of 354 identical discrete units of prefabricated concrete, arranged in such a way that every home has at least one private terrace.

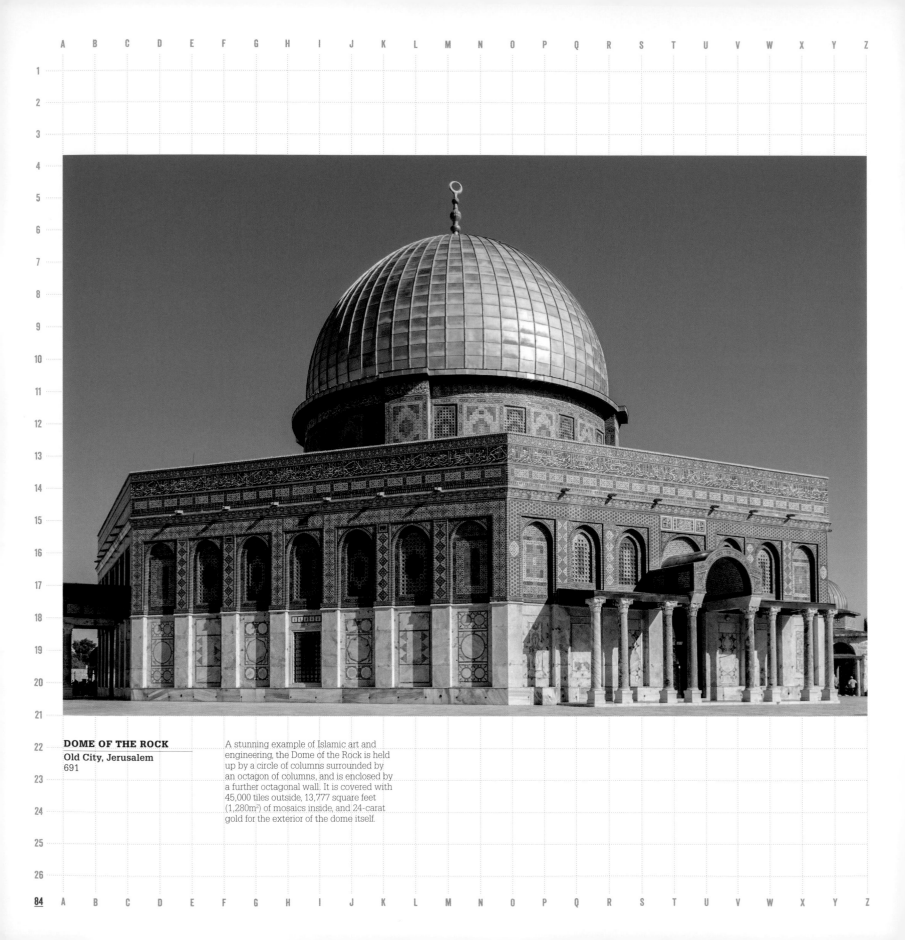

DOME OF THE ROCK

Old City, Jerusalem
691

A stunning example of Islamic art and engineering, the Dome of the Rock is held up by a circle of columns surrounded by an octagon of columns, and is enclosed by a further octagonal wall. It is covered with 45,000 tiles outside, 13,777 square feet (1,280m²) of mosaics inside, and 24-carat gold for the exterior of the dome itself.

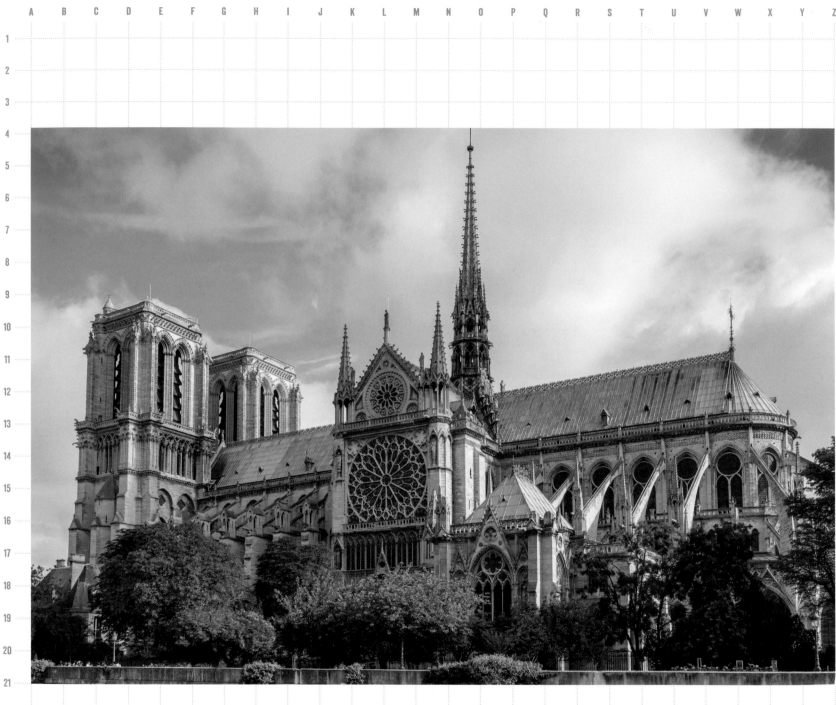

NOTRE-DAME

Paris, France
1163–1345

This landmark French Gothic cathedral was one of the first cathedrals to use flying buttresses—the support structures extending from the tall walls on either side. These buttresses, originally developed in late antiquity, were rediscovered by necessity, as a solution to the fractures that developed when lateral forces pushed the walls outward.

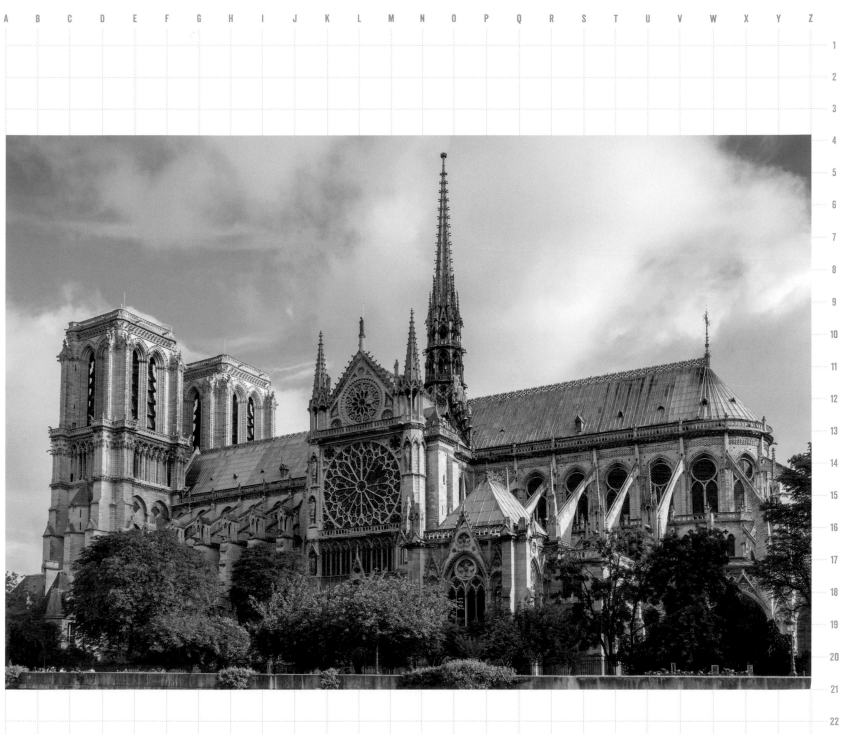

ANSWERS

P8
ROKUON-JI
Kyoto, Japan

B16, H10, J14, K6, M4, M9, M12, M17, M5, M7, O12, P2, Q15, R4, Q12, S6, S10, S12, T9, V11

P10
PAINTED LADIES
San Francisco, USA

A10, C19, D13, F17, H11, J10, L15, M14, M19, M8, N17, N18, O12, Q10, Q18, S10, T13, T14, W10, Y21

P12
CHURCH OF SAINT FRANCIS OF ASSISI
Ouro Preto, Brazil

G16, G18, H10, I4, J9, M23, N8, N15, O6, O11, O12, P18, P24, Q22, Q23, Q25, R17, R24, U10, V16

P14
TOPKAPI PALACE
Istanbul, Turkey

A7, B9, B15, E17, F18, G12, H21, J17, K18, M16, N5, P12, Q10, Q13, T6, V5, V8, V9, Y15, Y16

P16
FORBIDDEN CITY
Beijing, China

D21, E6, F10, G13, I19, K14, L8, L17, M15, M16, N6, N12, P8, P18, Q14, R15, V18, W15, X13, Y9

P18
SAINT PETER'S BASILICA
Vatican City

C12, E16, F14, I15, I16, J17, J20, L19, M6, M8, M11, N20, P19, R13, S14, S15, V15, V19, X15, Y10

P20
PALACE OF VERSAILLES
Versailles, France

B14, C8, D17, D7, F5, F10, G14, H7, M4, M8, M6, M7, M10, M18, Q9, R9, S6, T7, T9, W14

P22
CHRYSLER BUILDING
New York City, USA

G17, H24, I10, K9, K17, O4, O8, O16, O21, Q11, Q18, R14, R10, S11, S20, R21, T23, U14, U24, V18

P24
LAS LAJAS SANCTUARY
Ipiales, Colombia

H21, I17, K16, L22, M14, O17, O22, P11, Q3, Q8, R18, R20, T10, S13, U8, U17, W10, W13, X16, X4

P26
FLINDERS STREET STATION
Melbourne, Australia

B16, C19, C11, E7, H8, H16, K13, K18, L4, L16, L18, M15, N10, N12, P13, Q8, R13, R18, T7, T18

P28
SAINT BASIL'S CATHEDRAL (CATHEDRAL OF VASILY THE BLESSED) Moscow, Russia

G19, G20, I22, I16, J19, K19, K13, L22, N11, N13, N16, O5, O12, O15, N19, P21, S18, S22, T15, T16

P30
NEUSCHWANSTEIN CASTLE
Bavaria, Germany

H11, I11, J10, L7, N9, N18, M10, M20, O15, P11, R9, R13, R15, R18, S14, S19, T15, T17, U15, X2

P32
TAJ MAHAL, INDIA
Agra, India

B19, D16, E7, F16, H11, I11, K11, K12, K14, M6, M15, M15, M20, P11, P13, R11, R13, R14, V8, W16

P34
ELIZABETH TOWER,
PALACE OF WESTMINSTER
London, UK

K12, K14, K17, K20, L23, L16, N14, N15, N16, N18, N23, O2, O6, N8, O16, P25, Q9, R12, S17, T16

P36
PARIS LAS VEGAS
Las Vegas, USA

A14, B18, C13, C16, C20, E7, H6, I13, K16, N12, N20, R18, R19, S14, T13, T17, T19, X11, X14, Y15

P38
SHAH-I-ZINDA MAUSOLEUM
Samarkand, Uzbekistan

D14, E17, F12, G18, H12, I19, L11, L12, N13, N14, O12, O16, P19, R13, R16, T14, U11, W12, Y10, Y15

P40
INNTEL HOTEL ZAANDAM
Zaandam, The Netherlands

C10, C4, E11, F15, I16, J12, K2, K8, M5, M3, N16, Q20, Q6, S12, V5, V6, X6, Y8, Y12, Y15

P42
PONTE VECCHIO
Florence, Italy

B18, C14, D12, F16, F17, H9, H16, H18, I14, J15, N16, O15, T14, U15, U16, V13, X13, X15, X19, Y18

P44
CASTELLO DI SAMMEZZANO
Reggello, Italy

B19, C10, F6, F14, I10, K11, K17, L13, M6, M10, M11, M15, O16, P12, P14, S12, S18, T6, W6, X20

P46
WAT BENCHAMABOPHIT (THE MARBLE TEMPLE)
Bangkok, Thailand

B5, B16, A20, H14, H16, I12, K6, M10, M11, M13, M16, O16, O20, Q17, R16, T15, T18, V14, X11, X16

P48
CENTRAL LIBRARY, NATIONAL AUTONOMOUS UNIVERSITY OF MEXICO
Mexico City, Mexico

A13, E17, F11, F19, I10, J14, J12, K9, K12, K15, L9, M10, M13, M15, N8, N12, P10, T19, X18, Y19

P50
PENA PALACE
Sintra, Portugal

B10, D14, F4, F17, G7, G8, K8, L13, M7, M15, N13, Q7, Q12, Q17, R4, R8, S10, V13, V15, X10

P52
CHÂTEAU DE CHAMBORD
Chambord, France

A12, E17, F6, H13, H17, I9, I15, K8, K17, M11, N9, O7, P8, Q13, S7, U7, V8, V15, X17, Y12

P54
WINTER PALACE
Saint Petersburg, Russia

B15, C13, D18, F18, H17, H15, J17, K18, M7, M9, M10, M12, M14, M16, R12, T10, V10, V15, X17, Y9

P56
CHURCH OF THE SAVIOR ON SPILLED BLOOD
Saint Petersburg, Russia

F22, I17, J7, K20, K22, L13, M10, M19, N12, P4,
P9, Q14, Q17, Q22, R14, T14, T19, U17, V14, V21

P58
CASA BATLLÓ
Barcelona, Spain

C16, D16, E19, F10, H9, H16, I1, I4, K19, N10, N13, Q7,
Q14, S9, S15, U13, V6, V9, V7, X16

P60
**FLORENCE DUOMO (CATHEDRAL
OF SAINT MARY OF THE FLOWER)**
Florence, Italy

D15, G15, H8, H14, I3, J18, J9, K12, K13, K16, M10, N16, N17, P12,
Q16, R15, T16, V13, W10, W6

P62
BARBICAN CENTRE
London, UK

B13, D3, D10, F10, I7, I14, J16, J9, K14, L5, L11, M10, O3,
P10, S3, S7, U6, V3, W17, X9

P64
HAGIA SOPHIA
Istanbul, Turkey

D20, E16, G5, F7, H11, I19, K12, K16, M3, M8, N1, O12,
O13, Q9, R4, S18, U7, U12, U18, W2

P66
BUQSHAN HOTEL
Khaila, Yemen

B12, B16, E9, F10, G7, K8, L9, M14, N12, N4, N17, Q16, R10,
S17, S19, V4, V10, V19, X16, Y19

P68
MYSORE PALACE
Mysore, India

F20, H3, H9, J9, J23, J25, K4, K12, K24, M7, N4, O19, P8, P10, Q16, R8, R25, S11, S9, V22

P70
JINGMING TOWER, SUMMER PALACE
Beijing, China

B11, C13, F7, G11, G17, H9, H12, J9, K1, K19, M7, P10, P12, P16, Q19, S9, S13, S18, W11, W14

P72
ALHAMBRA
Granada, Spain

C14, C15, G13, I11, I12, I13, K11, K12, K14, K8, K13, K15, L10, L11, N13, P12, P15, P13, Q16, V12

P74
SAINT MICHAEL'S GOLDEN-DOMED MONASTERY
Kiev, Ukraine

A19, E15, G20, H17, K19, M20, M3, M8, N13, N14, O17, P20, Q12, R13, R20, S16, S17, U19, W11, W18

P76
DANCING HOUSE
Prague, Czech Republic

G21, I10, K3, J9, K13, M21, N11, O10, Q19, R2, S8, S21, T14, T16, U21, V5, V11, X11, X17, Y14

P78
SHEIKH ZAYED GRAND MOSQUE
Abu Dhabi, UAE

B13, C20, D15, E15, I6, K12, M16, N12, O11, O15, R15, R12, R15, S18, T11, U12, V12, Y7, Y9, Y15

P80
SAINT MARK'S BASILICA
Venice, Italy

C17, D7, E11, E17, F12, I19, I10, J12, J20, K8, L8, L17, O10,
P3, R15, R11, V7, U9, W11, X12

P82
HABITAT 67
Montreal, Canada

C7, D15, D17, F15, G15, H9, I5, I14, K3, J10, L6, N11, O7, O14, Q3, S3, S9, U14, U19, W14

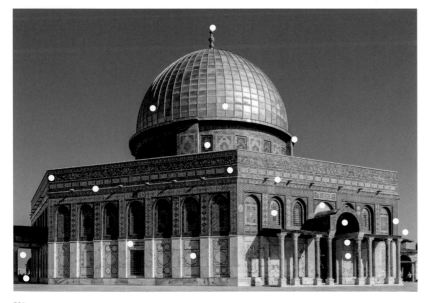

P84
DOME OF THE ROCK
Old City, Jerusalem

A19, A20, C14, F14, H18, I10, L19, M4, M12, N9, N13, Q14, Q16, R11, T15, U17, U18, U19, X16, Y17

P86
NOTRE-DAME
Paris, France

B18, C9, C15, D20, F14, G12, G13, K13, K14, K16, L12, M13, M14, O4, O17, P12, P15, R13, T13, X12